POEMS ABOUT THE GOSPEL II

Patrick McCaskey

Sporting Chance Press™, Inc.
1074 Butler Drive
Crystal Lake, IL 60014
sportingchancepress.com

Photographs appearing in *Poems About the Gospel II* were sourced from Fr. Lawrence Lew, O.P. Please see the Photo Credits table beginning on Page 163 for more information.

The opinions and ideas expressed are those of the author who is entirely responsible for its content. The author has composed *Poems About the Gospel II* at his own expense, using his own resources and technology. This publication is not associated in any way with the Chicago Bears Football Team.

CONTENTS

Poems About the Gospel II

LUKE

Poems About the Gospel II

Patrick McCaskey

Poems About the Gospel II

There are 150 Psalms. Here are 150 Poems about the Gospel.

Patrick McCaskey

God the Father

MATTHEW

Christ Had a Ministry in Galilee

Matthew 4:12-17, 23-25

Jesus proclaimed that the Kingdom of God
Had arrived. He was based in Capernaum
Which was next to the Sea of Galilee.
He preached there to fulfil the prophecies.

His call for repentance was quite urgent.
Penance would lead to changed hearts and lives.
God's word led to a kingdom perspective.
Acts of penance led to heavenly deeds.

With God's grace, we lose our lives to Jesus.
We put off the old; we put on the new.
Let what is spiritual prevail.
Rise from what is here to what is above.

Jesus Christ established the Kingdom of
God through His miracles and His preaching.

Jesus Christ Taught the Fullness of the Law

Matthew 5:17-19

Jesus did not want to replace the Law.
He wanted to bring it to perfection.
He explained the Law in general terms.
Then He established His authority.

God gave the Ten Commandments to Moses.
Jesus gave us the Eight Beatitudes.
That adds up to Eighteen which was Peyton
Manning's number. He is a great Christian.

This passage is from the Sermon on the
Mount, the greatest homily of all time.
I wasn't there, but I have typed it and
Timed it. It took about fifteen minutes.

Saint Augustine said the Sermon was "the
Perfect expression of the Christian life."

Upon Request, Jesus Taught the Lord's Prayer

Matthew 6:7-15

Jesus said to pray with sincerity.
To build up the body of the one Church.
In the Lord's Prayer, Jesus taught that there are
Seven petitions and seven blessings.

One, the name of God should be sanctified.
Two, the kingdom of God is on the way.
Three, God's love kingdom will fulfill His will.
Four, daily bread provides bodily strength.

Five, forgiveness of debts and offences
Leads to Six, protection from temptation
And Seven, deliverance from evil.
The Lord's Prayer summarizes the Gospel.

At a retreat, Fathers Mike Sparough and
Mike Rossman gave eight talks on the Lord's Prayer.

Patrick McCaskey

Let's Trust in God's Fatherly Providence

Matthew 6:24-34

God the Father feeds birds of the air.
He gives lilies of the field their beauty.
His daily protection never fails us.
He will provide what is necessary.

Christ told us to take each day as it comes.
Cut unnecessary anxiety.
The Kingdom of God is spiritual.
The world He maintains is material.

Here are two things for us to remember.
Finley Peter Dunne said, "Trust everybody,
But cut the cards." Jean Shepherd had a book
Called, "In God We Trust: All Others Pay Cash."

Sidney Poitier was a worker who
Built a chapel in "Lilies of the Field."

Jesus Taught Them

Jesus Told His Disciples How to Live

Matthew 7:1-5

Christ said practice fraternal charity,
And do not be out to condemn people.
Our sight can become distorted and see
Things in a bad light, even when they're fine.

Saint Augustine advised, "Try to acquire
Those virtues which you think your brothers lack."
When Abe Lincoln was mad at someone, he
Would write a letter and then not mail it.

My father, Ed McCaskey, used to say,
"When we are strong in an area in
Which others are weak, we are our brother's
Keeper." Brothers and sisters are helpful.

This may surprise you, but even I make
Mistakes. Brothers and sisters correct me.

Holy Things, Golden Rule, and Narrow Gate

Matthew 7:6, 12-14

What Christ taught was holy, a precious pearl.
Only the priests handle holy objects.
Those who believe in Transubstantiation
Can receive Catholic Holy Communion.

Regardless of what others do, we should
Love God and each other. That's the ticket.
Jackie Vernon said, "Do unto others,
Then cut out." The Golden Rule is quite cool.

Go through the narrow gate. Do not be late.
Worldly strife leads to everlasting life.
A pilgrimage is a worthwhile struggle.
While here on Earth, with my wife I'll snuggle.

Harry Kraemer says, "Be self-reflective.
Do the right thing and do the best you can."

Patrick McCaskey

Ravenous Wolves Like to Wear Sheep's Clothing

Matthew 7:15-20

Jesus said we would be judged on our works.
He warned us to beware of false prophets.
If they come from God, they will bear good fruit.
If they do not, then hang on to your loot.

False prophets lead the good people astray.
Jesus Christ is the way; what do you say?
Wheat with the chaff and have a hearty laugh.
You can't put sheep's clothing on a giraffe.

It's not enough to pray and go to Mass.
Let's be faithful like Job and Abraham.
Tribulation comes to every nation.
Work together without hesitation.

Jonathan Winters as Maude Frickert and
Flip Wilson as Geraldine were funny.

Christ Was Powerful and Self-Effacing

Matthew 8:1-4

Huge crowds followed Christ; He was popular.
A leper had faith in Christ who was modest.
Christ had mercy and respect for the Law.
All of us can learn from this episode.

Christ touched the leper with humility.
We must never scorn anyone for scars.
Let us not have leprosy of the soul.
If we repent, Jesus can make us clean.

I have had skin cancer three times. I'm cured.
Dermatology is helpful for me.
Sun block and a hat help prevent sunburn.
Doctor Michael Fretzin helps me to learn.

Jesus Christ did not want publicity.
He would later die for you and for me.

Christ Performed Miracles for the Faithful

Matthew 8:5-17

The centurion said that Christ was Lord.
Jesus acted with God's authority.
The Gospel was addressed to the whole world.
Miracles took place for people of faith.

The Roman officer had faith in Christ.
Jesus healed the centurion's servant.
The centurion had humility.
Christ humbled Himself to connect with us.

Faith plus humility equals reward.
After Christ cured Peter's mother-in-law,
She did not have a fever. She served Him.
After we're cured, let's serve God and others.

Christ took on the miseries of others.
His healings were wins over death and sins.

Christ Sent Evil Powers to the Showers

Matthew 8:28-34

Jesus was more powerful than demons.
The demons thought that Jesus was early.
It was not time for God's end victory.
Jesus Christ performed an exorcism.

A herd of pigs was eating heartily.
The demons asked to join them readily.
Jesus sent the demons obligingly.
Demons inside the pigs died instantly.

The herdsmen left the scene in a hurry.
It was too early to watch Steph Curry.
They told everything to everybody.
They asked Jesus to leave their neighborhood.

Teammate Ken Powers was a great leader.
He was dedicated and quite funny.

Christ Cured a Man
Who Had Been Paralyzed

Matthew 9:1-8

Jesus cured illnesses and the causes.
He performed miracles without pauses.
A paralyzed man was able to walk.
Some of the scribes had gossip in their talk.

They said that Jesus Christ was blaspheming.
They were inspired to begin their scheming.
The cheerleaders said, "Lean to the left, lean
To the right, stand up, sit down, fight, fight, fight."

Jesus forgave sins; the crowd was amazed.
Jimi Hendrix later sang "Purple Haze."
What Jesus Christ gave us was not a drug.
Thanks to Him we have a heavenly hug.

The power of Jesus Christ is divine.
If you want to be cured, please get in line.

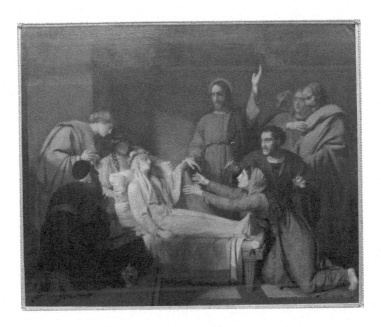

Christ Raises the Daughter of Jarius

Jesus Raised a Girl and Cured a Woman

Matthew 9:18-26

After the daughter of a ruler had
Died, he humbled himself before Jesus.
Jesus said she was not dead but sleeping.
After the laughter, He raised her to life.

A woman had suffered for twelve years, but
She believed in Jesus. If she could touch
His garment, she would be cured. She was right.

We get to receive Communion each day.
All we have to do is humble ourselves.
Then our faith in Christ will be rewarded.
When we need healing, show faith in Jesus.

In twenty eighteen, I had surgery
For prostate cancer. The surgery went
Well. I'm off the catheter and prune juice.

Christ Cured a Man and Called for Good Pastors

Matthew 9:32-38

Jesus cured a man who had been possessed.
Jesus proved that He was the Messiah.
The simple of heart saw His great power.
The twisted thinkers misinterpreted.

Matthew summarized the program of Christ.
The Apostles were sent to work God's fields.
The plight of the people moved Jesus Christ.
He preached the Gospel and worked miracles.

Christ called His disciples to do the same.
Go preach the Gospel before every game.
Do the best that you can for God's Glory.
His gifts make for a wonderful story.

We need more vocations for priests and nuns.
To do the work of God is more than fun.

Jesus Was an Excellent Recruiter

Matthew 10:1-7

God the Father sent Jesus Christ His Son.
Then Jesus Christ sent the twelve Apostles.
The twelve Apostles established the Church.
We have popes, cardinals, bishops, priests, and nuns.
Some of the clergy even go for runs.
Here's the Apostolic Starting Lineup:

83 Thomas	Left End
77 Philip	Left Tackle
66 Bartholomew	Left Guard
54 Seamus	Center
61 Thaddaeus	Right Guard
74 Simon	Right Tackle
87 Andrew	Right End
10 Peter	Quarterback
24 James	Left Halfback
44 Matthew	Fullback
21 John	Right Halfback
20 Judas	Kicker

Christ Gave Instructions to the Apostles

Matthew 10:16-23

Christ told the Apostles to bear witness.
They would be persecuted and betrayed.
The Holy Spirit would come to their aid.
They would have the great gift of martyrdom.

Apostles should not be disconcerted.
Their witnessing would all be for the best.
When they get to Heaven, they could all rest.
They would have proven their love of Jesus.

The Packers have thirteen championships.
The Bears have nine. This is disconcerting.
We are hopeful that the world will not end,
'Til the Bears have the most championships.

For a Martyr Contest, Mary said, "I
Didn't even know there was a contest."

Exhortations for All of the Nations

Matthew 10:24-33

The Apostles would be like Jesus Christ.
They would receive the same kind of slander.
The Apostles should "have no fear of them."
The Apostles should trust God's providence.

God does not abandon the little birds.
After they have seconds, they can have thirds.
Let there be no slander of the gander.
He takes awesome care of his family.

We should openly bear witness to God.
Even in a drought, He takes care of sod.
Jesus takes even greater care of us.
Better than Ralph Kramden, Christ drives the bus.

The Church spreads God's Kingdom throughout the
Earth.
While we are here, we can have some good mirth.

Sodom and Gomorrah, the Twin Cities

Matthew 11:20-24

Jesus preached and worked many miracles.
Loose living would earn divine punishment.
Christ drew attention to ingratitude.
The ungrateful would pay on Judgment Day.

This Matthew passage is not a lament.
There is time for all of us to repent.
After we have fallen into grave sin.
We have to rise up and try, try again.

Here is a David Steinberg joke. "Lot and
His wife fled Sodom and Gomorrah. Lot's
Wife said to him, 'Lot, what's the matter with
You? That was fun back there. How come you al-
ways do what God tells you to do?' Lot said,
'Dear, God told me to tell you to look back.'"

Christ Revealed His Father to the Humble

Matthew 11:25-27

Unbelievers of Jesus made Him sad.
Those who accepted Jesus made Him glad.
Humble folks did not trust their own wisdom.
They did not lean on their understanding.

Jesus Christ received everything from God.
Jesus recognized God as His Father.
Christ revealed God to the humble of heart.
In prayer, Jesus showed his deepest feelings.

Jesus always said Yes to His Father.
Jesus Christ expressed the depth of His heart.
He longed to give His Father good pleasure.
With love, He adhered His heart to God's will.

Sometimes I did not talk to my father.
He forgave me and we became great friends.

The Yoke of Jesus Christ is Not a Joke

Matthew 11:28-30

In Hosea, God announced that He would
Lead His faithful with compassion and love.
Jesus was the agent of God's movement.
The yoke is easy; the burden is light.

The burden of Jesus takes weight off you.
The burden of Christ gives you wings to fly.
Jesus is "gentle and lowly in heart."
Instead of anger, let's put trust in God.

Christ linked Himself to the wisdom he preached.
He decided to become perfect Man.
He loved us and He was most loveable.
He died for us; Ralph Kramden drove a bus.

Christ gave us the chance to get to Heaven.
Ralph offered to send Alice to the Moon.

Jesus Set the Pace for the Day of Rest

Matthew 12:1-8

The miracles of Jesus supported
His teaching. Jesus taught service to God
and neighbors do not break the Sabbath rest.
Sunday is not a day of rest for priests.

The merciful can see God and His works.
God would like to see His likeness in us.
Since we have received justice and mercy,
We should be just and merciful. Amen.

Since we were created in God's image,
He would like to see Himself in our hearts.
Our lives should imitate His works. Amen.
Our good works will always be rewarded.

If our ox falls into a ditch on a
Sunday, we should get it out on that day.

Jesus Tried to Avoid Confrontations

Matthew 12:14-21

Even in seclusion, Christ worked cures.
He was discreet; His mystery was key.
Jesus fulfilled Isaiah's prophecy.
Jesus Christ is the suffering Servant.

Jesus brought the light of the truth to the world.
His personage was gentle and discreet.
Humble Jesus would achieve victory.
He fulfilled the hopes of the believers.

John Perkins exemplified Jesus Christ.
John does not return evil for evil.
He left school after third grade. Now he has
Seventeen honorary doctorates.

John Perkins says, "Love is the final fight."
After we share, we receive so much more.

Patrick McCaskey

Jonah the Prophet; Jesus the Savior

Matthew 12:38-42

Jesus was asked for a miracle sign.
He foretold His death and resurrection.
He compared Himself to Prophet Jonah.
Jesus showed that He Himself was the sign.

Jesus was greater than Prophet Jonah.
Jesus was greater than King Solomon.
After death, Jesus Christ would rise again.
Jesus did it without any trash talk.

Kenny Loggins sang, "This Is It." "Are you
Gonna wait for a sign, your miracle?"
He encouraged his father to work out
After he had serious surgery.

Workouts are recess for the elderly.
Let's be glad for the opportunities.

Jesus Acknowledged His True Family

Matthew 12:46-50

The disciples of Jesus became His
Family. He helped them to be like Him.
Christ praised Mary because she did God's will.
Mary was obedient to God's Word.

She was a faithful guardian virgin.
She had no other natural children.
Disciples of Jesus are God's children.
Jesus does not show favoritism.

For a joke, my father, Ed McCaskey,
Said to many people, "You're my favorite."
For a prayer, my mother, Virginia H.
McCaskey, said, "I don't have a favorite."

I don't have a favorite child or grandchild.
I don't have a favorite book I've written.

Two Parables Help Us Get to Heaven

Matthew 13:44-46

Through parables Jesus described Heaven.
He also described how we can get there.
The hidden treasure means abundant gifts.
The pearl means Heaven is most beautiful.

A man found the treasure and then hid it.
A merchant found the pearl after a search.
The people concerned were quite generous.
God helps the people who work for His sake.

Here on Earth, we can follow Jesus Christ.
His death gave us the reward of Heaven.
The hidden treasure field had to be bought.
Jesus Incarnate is found everywhere.

To pay for the field we give up this world.
Then we enjoy the riches of Heaven.

Christ Did Not Have Honor in His Country

Matthew 13:54-58

At first, Jesus was a hometown hero.
Then He was subsequently rejected.
His Nazareth neighbors went dark on Him.
They did not believe His divinity.

Christ had a supernatural mission.
Their unbelief prevented miracles.
Christ had the power; they did not have faith.
They had the laundry, but not the ticket.

The carpenter's son could have the game won.
The fans in the stands had no marching bands.
Christ made ploughs and yokes and He told good
jokes.
Salvation symbols were not loud cymbals.

Christ gave us a good example of work.
All of His duties, Jesus did not shirk.

Patrick McCaskey

Beware of a Dance;
Saint John Had No Chance

Matthew 14:1-12

John the Baptist and Jesus were quite close.
John's death prefigured the death of Jesus.
We have hope in Christ; John's death is a win.
John was a just man. Heaven is the plan.

A terrible oath was sworn and fulfilled.
A prophet's head was not a just reward.
John's death was a Heavenly victory.
Saint John began his eternal journey.

Those who live as Christians get to Heaven.
What a great reward after death by sword.
Robert Lamm wrote a song called "Beginnings."
It's in "The Very Best of Chicago."

The day after my high school prom, I ran
The very best mile of my life, so far.

Jesus Christ Cured an Epileptic Boy

Matthew 17:14-20

Even after the Transfiguration,
The disciples had very little faith.
They could not cast a demon from a boy.
Christ could. He taught the importance of faith.

A very, very tiny mustard seed
Can become a bush that is ten-feet high.
If we are in union with Jesus Christ,
We share in the omnipotence of God.

Sincere powerful prayer can move mountains.
In everyday life, let us keep the faith.
May we be as constant as Max Planck.
He went from music to quantum physics.

I need help to understand Planck's constant.
Father Smyth taught me, "Never refuse help."

Christ Did Not Give Offence; He Paid Taxes

Matthew 17:22-27

Jesus taught His Disciples about His
Passion and Resurrection, and the Church.
They were upset about the Passion. They
Were consoled by Jesus and His power.

Jesus was not required to pay taxes
Because He was the Lord of the temple.
He told Peter to pay taxes to show
Respect and honor for authority.

Christ performed a miracle of a coin
In a fish and showed His kind providence.

Thanks to Steve Martin, we know how to be
A millionaire and never pay taxes.
"First, get a million dollars." When asked why
You never paid taxes, say "I forgot."

To Get to Heaven Become Like Children

Matthew 18:1-5, 10

The disciples asked Jesus who was the
Most important. He said a humble child.
There is no record of the disciples
Changing diapers or consoling babies.

Jesus liked to hang out with the humble.
The proud were well on their way to crumble.
Even the most successful would stumble.
The nature of a bee is to bumble.

Saint Augustine said that "the essential
Thing in the religion and discipline
Of...Christ" was "first, humility; second
Humility; and third, humility."

Amen. Charlotte wrote five words in her web:
"Some pig," "terrific," "radiant," "humble."

Fraternity, Authority, and Prayer

Matthew 18:15-20

Love your brother; correct him privately.
Quietly help him to the path of truth.
Repentance of sins leads to Communion.
Reconciliation leads to Heaven.

The Sacrament of Penance is helpful.
When we name our sins, the priest forgives us.
We are forgiven for serious sins.
John Paul II "Misericordia Dei"

Jesus is present in the Sacraments.
He is the one who really baptizes.
He speaks when Scripture is read in the Church.
He is present when the Church prays and sings.

He is there when two are there in His name.
Let's hear it for small group Bible Studies.

Four Hundred Ninety Times for Forgiveness

Matthew 18:21-35

Peter asked Jesus how many times did
He have to forgive his brother, seven?
Jesus replied, seventy times seven.
That works out to four hundred ninety times.

Jesus said that we should always forgive.
We need to receive and grant forgiveness.
We forgive because we are in God's debt.
God gives infinite mercy to sinners.

After a servant had received forgiveness,
For a large debt, he became hard-hearted.
He did not forgive small debts of others.
He found it quite difficult to forgive.

Grandpa Halas lived to be eighty-eight
And he said, "Life is too short for grudges."

Jesus Showed His Affection for Children

Matthew 19:13-15

Christ blessed the children who were brought to Him.
He laid His hands on them and prayed for them.
The disciples did not understand Christ.
Then Jesus Christ did something quite special.

He spoke His attitude with eloquence.
If you live with childlike simplicity,
You belong to the Kingdom of Heaven.
We can learn a lot from Christ and children.

Let's give piggyback rides while we're able.
It's more fun than horses from a stable.
Swing sets with a slide are a lot of fun.
Time with children is a game to be won.

Children and grandchildren are a blessing.
The movie "Jesus" has Debra Messing.

Jesus Christ Conversed with a Rich Young Man

Matthew 19: 16-22

The rich young man had kept the commandments.
He asked Jesus what good deed he should do.
The Boy Scouts had not been invented yet.
The Boy Scouts would do a good deed daily.

Jesus lovingly obeyed His Father.
For Heaven, Christ was detached from all things.
The rich young man went away very sad.
He did not respond to self-surrender.

Right after a Notre Dame College Prep
Baccalaureate Mass a man said to
Me, "If I had your money, I'd burn mine."
The Bears are untappable equity.

My goal is still to keep the Bears in the
Family until the Second Coming.

Patrick McCaskey

Christ Taught His Disciples About Riches

Matthew 19:23-30

Pete said the disciples left everything.
Jesus said they would receive even more.
Jesus on His throne will not be alone.
His followers will be with Him on thrones.

The so-called nondescript will be the first.
Gifts will be multiplied a hundredfold.
Cardinal George used to say, "If you give
To the poor, you won't have to go to Hell."

Follow Christ; show belief in a new world.
"New World" was the official newspaper
Of the Archdiocese of Chicago.
Sell subscriptions; get a day off from school.

In nineteen sixty-six, I was the "New
World" All-Area quarterback. Amen.

The Parable of the Vineyard Workers

Matthew 20:1-16

Christ taught the goodness and mercy of God.
Jesus went far beyond human justice.
All of us benefit from God's goodness.
Working in the vineyard is a blessing.

God is quite just. Paul Just played basketball.
Let's be grateful he played for Notre Dame.
Regardless of when God calls, let's say yes.
When He will call is anybody's guess.

Instead of accusing employers of
Acting wrongly, Jesus said don't judge God.
Accept the gifts of God; also thank Him
For involvement in His salvation plan.

When my grandfather negotiated, this
Was the parable that he like to use.

The Mother of the Sons of Zebedee

Matthew 20:17-28

Jesus predicted His passion and death.
He would be degraded and crucified.
He prepared the Apostles for their deaths.
They would share in Jesus' resurrection.

The mother of the sons of Zebedee
Wanted one son to sit at His right hand
And the other to sit at His left hand.
This did not sit well with all the others.

Jesus Christ did not impose His power.
The most humble became the first of all.
Saint Peter called priests to shepherd the flock.
Saint Paul was a servant to everyone.

King Herod decapitated Saint James.
Saint John died on the island of Patmos.

Christ Berated the Scribes and Pharisees

Matthew 23:1-12

Christ spoke to the crowd and His Disciples.
He did not like those scribes and Pharisees
Who were more concerned about their image
Than in living lives of integrity.

Christ did not want to abolish the Law.
He wanted to bring it to perfection.
Scribes and Pharisees preached but did not practice.
They sought the highest civic positions.

Jesus Christ was here to serve not be served.
He called His Disciples to be humble.
Here's something from Saint Augustine, "We are
Leaders and servants: we lead when we serve."

Faith based writers and leaders need to teach
And preach about the Kingdom of heaven.

Patrick McCaskey

Jesus Expressed Woes to the Hypocrites

Matthew 23:13-32

Excessive worry about unclean gnats
Leads to blindness about impure camels.
Anyone who is always on a stage
Could become a phony at any age.

Hypocrites try to look good to others.
They're not funny like the Smothers Brothers.
Dick asked, "If someone told you to jump off
A bridge, would you?" Tom replied, "Not again."

Since we are made in God's image, we should
Imitate God: justice, mercy, and faith.
Seek fulfillment in God, the best reward.
Do not abolish the Law; enhance it.

If we pout or shout, we need a time out.
Quiet time is helpful to be sublime.

Saint John Chrysostom

Patrick McCaskey

The Parable of the Faithful Servant

Matthew 24: 42-51

Jesus did not reveal when Judgment Day
Will come. He wants us to be vigilant.
Instead of looking for signs, let us live
Our lives at all times in a Christian way.

The faithful servant is always on time.
When he gives food, he helps us feel sublime.
When the master is at home or away,
The servant is reliable every day.

Saint John Chrysostom helps us. "If you ex-
amine your conscience every day, you may
Go with confidence to the court of justice to which all go in fear and trembling."

My grandfather called the people who worked
On most Saturdays, the Saturday Crew.

The Parable of the Many Talents

Matthew 25:14-30

Jesus Christ wants us to respond to grace.
We should do it for the rest of our lives.
All of the gifts of God should bear their fruit.
We should always put our gifts to good use.

Serve other souls and all society.
Killing time on Earth is killing Heaven.
Do not back out of things and hide away.
Love God and give yourself to Jesus Christ.

Our lives are for God and for everyone.
Let's not bury our talents; make them yield.
Talents are gifts from God. Let's constantly
Exert ourselves to produce good results.

My talents are writing and performing.
God has been very, very good to me.

Patrick McCaskey

The Preparations for the Last Supper

Matthew 26:14-25

The Passover was a celebration
Of liberation from slavery in
Egypt. Moses had said an unblemished
Lamb should be sacrificed and then eaten.

When Jesus was here, lamb was sacrificed
In the Temple of Jerusalem. Then meals
Took place in the homes of people who had
Gathered together for celebration.

Unleavened bread was also served because
The Israelites took that from Egypt.
He had His Disciples say to a man
They would have Passover at the man's house.

Jesus knew that He was the Lamb who would
Later be sacrificed for our salvation.

The Great Commission Was Not Sedition

Matthew 28:16-20

Jesus Christ is God and omnipotent.
He has dominion, glory, and kingdom.
He gave His Apostles a commission.
They were to baptize and teach salvation.

Instead of being servant in Heaven
The devil chose to be ruler in Hell.
We were made in God's image. Jesus Christ
Died for our sins. The Spirit inspires us.

In a James Thurber "New Yorker" cartoon,
An angry man said to a woman, "I
Assume then, that you regard yourself as
Omniscient. If I am wrong, correct me!"

Knute Rockne used to say, "Keep on the balls
Of your feet. Then you'll look like something neat."

45

Patrick McCaskey

Annunciation Sculpture

MARK

The Baptism of Jesus, Son of God

Mark 1:7-11

John the Baptist was the last prophet and
First witness to Jesus the Messiah.
Baptist John felt that he was unworthy
To untie the sandal straps of Jesus.

John said that Christ was "mightier than I."
Today he might have said "I've got a guy."
John baptized with water and he said that
Christ would baptize with the Holy Spirit.

God the Father said that Jesus was His
Beloved Son in whom He was well pleased.
The Holy Spirit appeared in the form
Of a dove like the dove on Noah's ark.

I have three sons in whom I am well pleased.
One works for the Bears and two are experts.

Jesus Preached and Called His First Disciples

Mark 1:14-20

After John the Baptist was arrested,
Jesus preached about the Kingdom of God.
People who want to have a share in it
Need a conversion and an acceptance.

Christ called Simon and his brother Andrew.
Jesus Christ called James and his brother John.
And they responded immediately.
The Disciples left everything behind.

After Jesus had risen from the dead,
The Apostles echoed Jesus' preaching.
Thanks to the great Apostles, we have the
Sacrament of Reconciliation.

When my mother asks me to do something,
I say, "I'll do that next." And then I do.

Saint Augustine

Patrick McCaskey

Christt Taught
in the Capernaum Synagogue

Mark 1:21-28

After Christ had arrived in Capernaum,
He went to the synagogue and He taught.
The people were astonished because He
Taught with authority, unlike the scribes.

The preaching of Jesus was powerful.
He had the power to command demons.
What Jesus Christ preached was the word of God.
He ordered the possessed man to be free.

From Saint Augustine, we know that "These words
Show that the unclean spirits were possessed
Of great knowledge and were wholly lacking
In love." They don't "see and love his justice."

Since I have quite limited knowledge,
My goal is to be a lifelong learner.

Jesus Cured People;
Then He Prayed Alone

Mark 1:29-39

After Jesus had left the synagogue,
He went into Simon and Andrew's home.
Because Simon's mother-in-law had a
Fever, Jesus cured her. Then she served them.

Jesus Christ worked miracles quite often.
He cured human suffering with power.
He told the disciples to be quiet.
Jesus wanted to be known by His cross.

The next day, Jesus got up early to pray.
In prayer He learned to serve many others.
Instead of staying in that area,
Jesus preached in many, many places.

My mission is to write essays and poems
And then record them for WSFI.

Patrick McCaskey

Christ Called Matthew to Be a Disciple

Mark 2:13-17

After Jesus had taught all of a crowd,
He saw Levi. Jesus said, "Follow me."
Levi left the tax office and followed.
Christ, Levi, and others had a banquet.

A shared meal showed friendship and great respect.
This was a meal with tax men and sinners.
All who repent can obtain Salvation.
Jesus Christ did not exclude anyone.

All of us can change and become better.
That's why Saint Paul sent many a letter.
God's mercy can obtain us forgiveness.
Then we can pray for those bent on sinning.

Christ said eternal life was a banquet.
Let banquets be a preview of heaven.

Jesus Led a Discussion on Fasting

Mark 2:18-22

Jesus and His Disciples did not fast.
When people criticized them, Jesus Christ
Gave the example of the bridegroom. He
Implied that He was more than a teacher.

In the Old Testament, husband was
Used as an image of the Messiah.
Jesus as a bridegroom is the cause of
Great joy. Let there be dancing in the streets.

The Law was made whole and faith was perfect.
Jesus fulfilled all of the prophecies.
He said that the bridegroom would be taken.
It was a reference to His passion.

Christ gave us a vision of joy and sorrow.
Heaven will give us a great tomorrow.

Patrick McCaskey

Jesus Christ Taught the Law of the Sabbath

Mark 2:23-28

When Jesus let His Disciples eat grain
On the Sabbath, He saw their basic need.
They were hungry and they needed to eat.
Grain was an extraordinary treat.

In David's time, there were twelve loaves on the
Temple table from twelve Israel tribes.
When the priests replaced the old loaves with new,
They were allowed to eat the un-fresh loaves.

Lesser rules gave way to important ones.
Jesus restored the law of Sabbath rest.
On the Sabbath we give glory to God.
On Sunday, we celebrate Christ risen.

Jesus said He was Lord of the Sabbath.
His argument implied that He was God.

Christ Cured Beside the Sea of Galilee

Mark 3:7-12

Christ preached the Gospel and worked miracles.
He drew crowds from all over Palestine.
When He went to the Sea of Galilee,
His Disciples rescued Him in a boat.

The crowd could not crush Jesus from the shore.
His ministry was much more than folklore.
Contact with Jesus led to salvation.
Wonderful news spread to every nation.

From Saint Clement, we know that Jesus Christ
Raised our eyes to heaven and we see God.
Jesus Christ opened the eyes of our heart.
Jesus Christ filled our dark, dull minds with light.

He gave us knowledge of eternity.
Through Jesus, we can have serenity.

Christ's Relatives Were Concerned About Him

Mark 3:20-21

After Jesus Christ had chosen His twelve
Disciples, He went home. A crowd followed.
It was not possible to eat. After
That, Perry Como sang "It's Impossible."

Families of Old Testament prophets
Worried about excessive ministry.
Relatives of Christ had the same concern.
Christ made the effort because He loved us.

Many saints have followed Christ's example.
Holy Communion is a great sample.
Good banquets are secular communion.
Loaves and fishes make a tasty union.

Let us all have tuna on rye without
The contamination of celery.

Jesus Told Us About His True Kinsmen

Mark 3:31-35

Some relatives of Christ thought He was mad.
Jesus' true kinsmen did the will of God.
Mary set the pace for Christ's disciples.
She responded to God's will quite quickly.

From Saint Augustine, we know that Mary
Was chosen to give birth to Jesus Christ.
She was His mother and His disciple.
She fulfilled the Father's will perfectly.

Mary did not have any other children.
The Son of God the Father was plenty.
Saint Matthew wrote that the brothers of Christ
Were the sons of yet another Mary.

Doctor Jessen said I was his son. Bill
Wade said I was his spiritual son.

The Parables Are About God's Kingdom

Mark 4:1-20

The Kingdom of God has strength and victory.
Parables lead to faith development.
The sower parable is a partial.
Other parables are necessary.

Jesus was present and He preached quite well.
What is our disposition and response?
The words of Jesus were a mystery.
He explained them to His twelve Disciples.

If we know Jesus Christ and His mission,
We can understand His perfect preaching.
Jesus gave instruction to His Disciples.
He had chosen them to go out and preach.

We have the freedom to accept God's grace.
Then we too can preach through words and actions.

Jesus Made the Wind and Sea Obey Him

Mark 4:35-41

Jesus Christ showed that He had God's power.
Since He dominated the elements,
He gave the earth a heavenly order.
Faith in Jesus leads to tranquility.

Because of Saint Augustine, we know that
"Christ is asleep in your boat. Wake Him up,
And He will calm the storm and your fears...
Remember your faith; wake Christ within you."

Flavia Passarelli said to my
Sister, Anne, "You were born on a stormy
Night. So, I'm a gonna call you Stormy."
Many people called it a perfect storm.

My father, Ed McCaskey, used to say,
"Take care of yourself. Good people are scarce."

Patrick McCaskey

Christ Cured a Woman
and Restored a Girl

Mark 5:21-43

Belief and knowledge of Christ has power.
The woman with the hemorrhage was bold.
She was desperate; she touched Christ's garments.
After Christ had cured her, He talked with her.

He let her know the cure was not magic.
The miracle was from God Almighty.
The daughter of Jairus was quite near death.
Jairus believed that Jesus could help her.

Jesus encouraged the faith of Jairus.
The crowd at the house laughed at Jesus Christ.
He did not say, "Tough crowd." He restored her.
She was brought back to life and earthly strife.

Christ performed these miracles quietly.
He did not do them for publicity.

Homecoming for Jesus Was Not Pleasant

Mark 6:1-6

When Christ went to his hometown Nazareth,
He talked to a hostile synagogue crowd.
What He said astonished his old neighbors.
They did not expect wisdom from Jesus.

Jesus had been a family craftsman.
He and His neighbors had the same lifestyle.
The childhood of Jesus was hidden.
Everyday life led to His holiness.

Henny Youngman would have said, "Take my wife,
Please. Laugh it up. These are the jokes. I know
You're out there because I hear you breathing.
Is this an audience or a painting?"

A director wrongly once said to me,
"It is never the audience's fault."

Patrick McCaskey

Jesus Had a Universal Mission

Mark 6:7-13

After the Disciples had internships
With Jesus, He sent them out two by two.
They echoed the preaching of Jesus Christ.
They traveled from one place to the next one.

They had power over unclean spirits.
Like Jesus, they had a mixed reception.
Jesus emphasized detachment from things.
They did not need to wear expensive rings.

After the Disciples had anointed
The sick with oil, many people were cured.
Jesus instituted the Sacrament
Of Extreme Unction which I have received.

John Bostrom of the Bears was an intern.
He has said, "Interns are human forklifts."

The Apostles Returned to Jesus Christ

Mark 6:30-34

When the Apostles returned to Jesus,
They told Him about what they had finished.
Jesus told them to go away and rest.
He was grateful that they had done their best.

Jesus and the Apostles were busy.
They were dedicated to saving souls.
Leisure to eat was not one of their goals.
They did go by themselves on a boat ride.

The crowd saw the Apostles and followed them.
The crowd ran ahead and they got there first.
Jesus saw the crowd and felt compassion.
He became their shepherd and He taught them.

If we have had rest, we can do our best.
My dad used to say, "There's work to be done."

Loaves and Fishes for Five Thousand, To Go

Mark 6:34-44

Jesus saw that the crowd was leaderless.
So, He had compassion for them. He taught
Them. He gave them loaves and fishes to eat.
This was a fulfilment of prophecies.

The disciples wanted to send the crowd
Away. Jesus said to feed them today.
Groups of fifty and a hundred sat to-
gether. They probably had good weather.

Jesus was a shepherd. He guided and
Provided. This prefigured Communion.
He gave more than was needed. He wanted
All the leftovers to be collected.

Jesus taught us not to waste our talents.
We can receive Communion every day.

Jesus Walked on Water, Not a Treadmill

Mark 6:45-52

Jesus worked miracles to show that He
Was the Messiah. He had great power.
Jesus came to His Disciples at dawn.
It was much too early to mow the lawn.

Christ allowed His Disciples to suffer.
He did not help them immediately.
He let them be in danger all night long.
Tribulation taught them to be patient.

When we are under a lot of pressure,
Jesus is always around to help us.
When we make an effort to work it out,
He strengthens our hope. We are resilient.

Avoid being ill, walk on a treadmill.
Here's to four miles a day. What do you say?

Jesus Christ Cured
a Greek Woman's Daughter

Mark 7:24-30

Jesus went away to hide in a house.
That was not possible, even for Him.
A Greek woman from Syrophoenicia
Had a little daughter who was possessed.

The Greek woman had heard about Jesus.
She found Him and she "fell down at His feet."
She pleaded with Christ to cure her daughter.
Jesus preached salvation for everyone.

Christ did not say, "It would be hard to put
Syrophoenicia on a jersey."
They had a wonderful conversation.
Jesus cured the woman's daughter from there.

If we offer prayers with humility
And perseverance, God will hear our prayers.

Jesus Christ Multiplied the Loaves Again

Mark 8:1-10

A great crowd was with Jesus for three days.
They had come from afar to hear Him preach.
He did not want them to go home hungry.
If the crowd would faint, it would not be quaint.

In the beginning there were seven loaves.
After everyone had an excellent
Sufficiency, there were seven baskets
Of leftovers. There were loaves for take home.

Jesus instituted the Sacrament
Of Communion which I receive daily.
I need God's grace to prepare for my race:
Four hundred meters as fast as I can.

Salvation is for every nation.
God Almighty is a great sensation.

Patrick McCaskey

Sign from Heaven and Dough Rise from Leaven

Mark 8:11-13

The Pharisees had a bad disposition.
They asked Jesus for a sign from heaven.
They expected more than rise from leaven.
They made it feel like an inquisition.

The Disciples had many shortcomings.
They would rather talk more than do something.
After the Apostles had been filled with
The Holy Spirit, they were Church pillars.

The miracles and resurrection of
Christ were signs that He was the Messiah.
On many occasions of epiphany,
My Grandma Kit used to say, "It's a sign."

To understand Christ be spiritual.
During the pandemic be virtual.

Christ Said No to the Pharisees' Leaven

Mark 8:14-21

The Pharisees and Herod did not see
The meaning of the signs of Jesus Christ.
If they had been playing baseball, they would
Have shaken off the signs. They would have lost.

Five loaves of bread for five thousand people
Led to twelve baskets of leftover bread.
Seven bread loaves for four thousand people
Led to seven baskets of leftovers.

Christ risen is like the sign of Jonah.
It was not meant to be a spectacle.
The Apostles went fishing for people.
They were dispensers of the grace of God.

Instead of eating much earthly leaven,
Perry Como sang "Pennies from Heaven."

Patrick McCaskey

Peter Acknowledged Jesus as the Christ

Mark 8:27-35

Jesus Christ is humble and powerful.
Jesus Christ is the suffering Servant.
Jesus accepted the cross for Himself.
Every Christian must follow Jesus Christ.

Jesus Christ taught His disciples the true
Nature of His mission: salvation through
Suffering and the cross. The followers
Of Christ must renounce their wills and desires.

The Cross is a symbol of victory.
God is more beautiful than the planet.
Love God more than the world He created.
God gave us the world so we would love Him.

My uncle, Bob Wolff, used to say, "I'm all
Alone at the foot of the Cross." Amen.

Three Disciples Saw Jesus Transfigured

Mark 9:2-10

After Christ had led Peter, James, and John
Up a high mountain, He was transfigured.
His garments became very, very white.
They had not been bleached but they gave off light.

Elijah and Moses talked with Jesus.
Peter said three booths should be made for them.
The three Disciples were very frightened.
Then a big voice from a cloud spoke to them.

God the Father told the Disciples to
Listen to His beloved Son, Jesus.
The Disciples did not understand what
They saw and heard. It was a mystery.

Coach Cole used to say, "Every time there is
A vote in the huddle, the linemen win."

Patrick McCaskey

Jesus Taught His Disciples Privately

Mark 9:30-37

The disciples did not understand Christ.
With God's grace, they would understand later.
The prophets had foretold what Jesus taught.
He would suffer death in Jerusalem.

This was the only way to save mankind.
Christ only told the disciples about it.
Christ told the disciples to be servants.
They were not to be the Church taskmasters.

Then they would be equipped to be leaders.
Ambition and pride should be put aside.
A desire to control others leads to
Many unhappy sisters and brothers.

Let's serve everybody with charity.
The world is much more than just you and me.

A Rich Young Man Says No to Poverty

Mark 10:17-27

Christ called a rich young man to follow Him.
Unlike the first disciples, he said no.
Material things can become false gods.
When we know and love God, we can say yes.

It's important to keep a low profile.
I have the least expensive Cadillac.

My goal is to keep the Bears in the fam-
ily until The Second Coming. In
The meantime, I shall continue to tithe.
I'll also save to pay estate taxes.

When I started working for the Bears, my
Hair was brown, curly, and thick. Now my hair
Is white, straight, and thin. God is protecting
My marriage. I was too good looking.

Followers of Jesus Get to Heaven

Mark 10:28-31

Peter said to Jesus, "Lo, we have left
Everything and followed you." Jesus said
In effect, "You are going to get a
Great rebate. You get to go to Heaven."

Jesus said they would be persecuted.
When offered for Christ, they would receive joy.
When we hear God call us to holiness,
Let us answer with alacrity, yes.

The Saint Mary's cheerleaders sang, "one, two,
Three, four, five, six, seven, all good players
Go to Heaven. When they get there they re-
peat, Saint Mary's, Saint Mary's, can't be beat."

Dionne Warwick sang, "You'll Never Get
To Heaven If You Break My Heart." Amen.

No Figs and a House of Prayer for Jesus

Mark 11:11-26

Christ was hungry for a fig; there were none.
So, Jesus Christ cursed the barren fig tree.
The Disciples heard it and could not help.
Fig Newtons had not been invented yet.

Jesus Christ cleansed the temple of robbers.
The thieves left. It became a place of prayer.
Purification for every nation,
Prayer with the right inner disposition.

Do not approach God in prayer with rancour.
Pray with charity in a faith spirit.
Jesus knows our needs, even fig tree seeds.
If it bleeds, it leads, does not apply here.

Saint Teresa of Avila said to
Pray to God since He will not fail to give.

Patrick McCaskey

The Authority of Christ Was Questioned

Mark 11:27-33

After Jesus Christ had cleansed the temple,
He was asked to explain his behavior.
He had already proved that He was God.
John the Baptist had also confirmed it.

Christ was ready to have a dialogue,
But He confronted them with a question.
Did they accept John as Christ's Precursor?
If they accept John, then they accept Christ.

They were not ready to acknowledge John.
This led to their spiritual blindness.
They were afraid of people and truth. Is
He or isn't He? That was the question.

Attempts to call God to account are not
Escapes from ignorance and confusion.

Jesus Christ Taught Us to Pay Our Taxes

Mark 12:13-17

During the two thousand eight preseason,
I was asked who will start at quarterback.
I said, "Rend to Lovie the things that
Are Lovie's, to God the things that are God's."

Tax time is the most tedious time of
The year. With the tax people working, and
The IRS lurking it's hard to cheer.
It's the most tedious time of the year.

There's a deadline for filing, not much time
For smiling and wistfully watching the
Snow. There'll be scary tax stories, tales of
The glories of deadlines met long ago.

There'll be no double filing and may-
be some smiling when the deadline is near.

The Sadducees Tried
to Trap Jesus Christ

Mark 12:18-27

Christ showed the Sadducees where they went wrong.
They tried to reduce the greatness of God,
The human mind has limitations.
There's no limit to God's benevolence.

They underestimated God's power.
They tried to find contradictions in the
Holy Scripture. They lacked humility.
Huey Lewis sang, "The Power of Love."

Saint Hippolytus gave us great advice.
There is only one God, my brothers, and
We can come to know him only through the
Holy Scripture. Therefore, we must strive to
Understand the things that we are told in
The Scriptures" and then do what we are taught.

The Divinity of the Messiah

Mark 12:35-37

Peter said Jesus was the Messiah.
Bartimaeus said Christ was David's son.
The multitudes said Jesus was the one.
Jesus Christ said He was the Son of God.

The scribes were a tough crowd; Christ was tougher.
Christ was a leader; He was a reader.
He read the Scriptures that His Father inspired.
Jesus Christ was a great public speaker.

Saint Hilary of Poitiers said the
Scribe "was ignorant of the Law and did
Not know that Christ must be acknowledged as"
...David's son "according to the Spirit."

Saint Hilary of Poitiers, France, was
A bishop and a doctor of the Church.

Patrick McCaskey

A Poem from a Former Patrol Boy

Mark 13:33-37

Jesus said that we should be vigilant.
From "Navarre" we know we must be vibrant.
This is a parable; let's be prepared.
It is not good for us to know the time,
Since we would only be good at the end.
Being faithful is our mountain to climb.

Jesus is the traveling householder.
Peter is the vigilant gatekeeper.
We're the servants who are here to wash feet.
Getting to Heaven would make us complete.
Our job is to obey the Commandments
In the Spirit of the Beatitudes.

We are the sentinels and the sentries.
Like patrol boys, let us be attentive.

A Kind Woman Anointed Jesus Christ

Mark 14:1-15

Since Jesus Christ was a distinguished guest,
A generous woman anointed Him
With perfumed water. He said that she did
Not make a mistake. Her critics were wrong.

Saint John Chrysostom pointed out that she
Did not do her good deed before a large crowd.
It did not take place where it could be seen.
The event took place in a private house.

My father made a grand exit. At the
End of an event, he used to say, "My
Wife and I are leaving. She needs time to
Give me a massage and to draw my bath."

The two-thousand-year-old man, Mel Brooks, said
The greatest invention was Liquid Prell.

Patrick McCaskey

The Last Supper Was the First Eucharist

Mark 14:12-16, 22-26

Christ had a great attention for detail.
He sent two of His disciples ahead.
They made elaborate preparations.
The Last Supper was a sumptuous meal.

Jesus knew what was going on: God's plan.
He knows what is going on in our lives.
Jesus knew that He was going to die.
We can all trust in God's redemptive plan.

Jesus Christ loves us. We have Communion.
Go to Church for a Last Supper reunion.
Jesus Christ gave bread to His disciples.
He also gave them wine on which to dine.

After Jesus had risen from the dead,
He did not taunt those who rejected Him.

A Poem About Mark Chapter Fifteen

Jesus did not deserve to die for sin.
Jack Benny said, "I don't really deserve
This award, but I have arthritis and
I don't deserve that either." Christ loved us.

Jesus the Son died for our salvation.
Jesus was mocked and scourged and crowned with
thorns.
The crucifixion led to salvation.
Jesus was righteous and persecuted.

Christ's divinity has been acknowledged.
Every nation can now worship the Lord.
Wonderful women ministered to Christ.
They loved Him and they were His witnesses.

Joseph of Arimathea was bold.
He asked Pilate for the body of Christ.

The Tomb Was Empty; Jesus Had Risen

Mark 16:1-7

Jesus of Nazareth was crucified.
Since He had risen, His tomb was empty.
Mark made certain that the person who was
Crucified/Risen was the same person.

Jesus Christ was the ultimate winner.
He defeated death, sin, pain, the devil.
The Disciples would be the witnesses.
They would be the Church originators.

The Church's mission was not sedition.
The world be in better condition.
The Good News was for every nation.
Everybody could obtain salvation.

Jesus rose from the dead on a Sunday.
That is a day when the Bears often play.

Mary Magdalene and the Disciples

Mark 16:9-15

They were not a rock group. They were the first
To see Jesus Christ after He had risen.
Christ appeared to Mary and two disciples.
Others suffered from incredulity.

When Jesus appeared to all eleven,
He gave them a mission. They accepted.
They would preach salvation to the whole world.
Baptism is the way to obtain it.

The other Sacraments are also helpful.
The Body of Jesus Christ is the Church.
We go to Church for His mediation.
He provides heavenly transportation.

Charity and respect for freedom guide
The Church to provide the heavenly truth.

Benediction

LUKE

The Circumcision of John the Baptist

Luke 1:57-66, 80

An angel had told Zechariah that
His son should be named John (the Baptist.)
John was born at home which was not in Rome.
Then Zechariah wrote, "His name is John."

The speech of Zechariah was restored.
His tongue was loosed; he believed in Our Lord.
John was the Precursor of Jesus Christ.
All of the prophecies became fulfilled.

In the year forty-nine, the Apostles
Replaced circumcision with Baptism.

My wife is Protestant; she married me.
I don't have the gift of celibacy.
Our sons were baptized and dedicated.
One is Protestant; two are Catholic.

Saint Joseph the Worker

Jesus Preached in His Hometown, Nazareth

Luke 4:14-22

When Christ was in Galilee synagogues,
All of His listeners glorified Him.
Then He went to teach in Nazareth, His
Hometown. The people there were a tough crowd.

First, He read from the Book of Isaiah.
Then He sat down and talked to His people.
They remembered Him as son of Joseph.
They did not see Him as the Messiah.

Jesus had been home schooled. He had daily
Recess, a perfect attendance record,
And no detentions. He was a perfect
Student. He was valedictorian.

The people of Nazareth were narrow-
minded. They did not accept Jesus Christ.

The Works of Jesus Christ Backed Up His Words

Luke 4:31-37

Jesus was much more than a quote machine.
The works that He did were really quite keen.
What He said resonates eloquently.
What He did gave Him credibility.

The devil is called the father of lies.
Soupy Sales frequently received face pies.
Jesus Christ told the demon to be quiet.
We need to be prudent and not riot.

Half-truths are lies, the devil in disguise.
A clean mouth is needed to speak the truth.
Let us give much praise to Esther and Ruth.
Let us receive God's will into our hearts.

Sports Faith International works because
Sports draw and then we sell the medicine.

Jesus Christ Cured Peter's Mother-in-Law

Luke 4:38-44

People asked Christ to help Peter's mother-
in-law because she had a high fever.
We learn prayer for others is effective.
Christ's compassion was not an elective.

Christ worked cures in a particular way.
"He laid his hands on every one of them."
Jesus took care of individuals.
He taught us have concern for everyone.

Jesus cured people immediately.
Jesus did not have anonymity.
The people wanted Jesus Christ to stay.
Other cities need Him to come their way.

Quiet life without strife is not for me.
I have a need to recite poetry.

Patrick McCaskey

Jesus Went Fishing for Disciples

Luke 5:1-11

When Peter, James, and John fished on their own,
Without Jesus, they were unsuccessful.
With Christ as their guide, the fish did not hide.
They jumped into the boat; they did not float.

From the Navarre Bible commentary,
Here is what I learned from the passage.
Remember the past with gratitude; live
The present with enthusiasm; look
Forward to the future with confidence.

"Like all those chosen by God for a mission,
Jesus said to Peter, "Do not be afraid."

My best lunch is tuna on rye, without
The contamination of celery
And a banana strawberry smoothie.

Jesus Christ Called Levi to Follow Him

Luke 5:27-32

When Jesus called Levi to follow Him,
It was not based on his tax collecting.
Jesus looked at Levi with eyes of love.
Levi was grateful, generous, and prompt.

Jesus asked Levi to be like Jesus.
Levi forgot about his earthly things.
Jesus Christ did not have any possessions.
He did have many blessings and lessons.

Jesus filled Levi's mind with a great grace.
The dining room table did not need lace.
The meal with Levi was quite a great feast.
Christ called him to give to those who had least.

Steven Wright said, "You can't have everything.
Where would you put it? Earth is bi-polar."

Patrick McCaskey

Jesus Reworked the Law of the Sabbath

Luke 6:1-5

Since David had eaten bread from God's House,
Jesus said His disciples could eat grain.
He said to the scribes and the Pharisees,
"The Son of Man is lord of the Sabbath."

Christ manifested his divine power
And authority. Jesus explained the
Right way to understand the Sabbath rest.
The small-minded doubt the greatness of God.

On a Saturday, I ran the fastest
Mile of my life, so far. On the next day,
I tried to beat that time: 4:37.9.
Perry Como sang, "Blame It on My Youth."

A day of rest would have been much better.
I still received a letterman's sweater.

Christin Cured a Man Who Had a Withered Hand

Luke 6:6-11

Long after Christ had cured a withered hand,
Professor Harold Hill led a boys' band.
The scribes and Pharisees were a tough crowd.
Compared to Jesus, they were way too loud.

There are people who seem to be heartless.
Tin Man from "The Wizard of Oz" had heart.
He was presuming he could be human.
He was tender, gentle, sentimental.

My father often imagined that his
Children were asking, "What are we going
To do with Pop?" We enjoyed his singing,
His stories, and his many kindnesses.

When I had two broken hands, Coach Willett
Said, "You don't run with your hands; stay in shape."

Jesus Christ Spoke
About Pure Intentions

Luke 6:43-49

We know the type of tree by the tree's fruit.
A tree with apples is an apple tree.
A person with good works has a good heart.
Let's surrender our will to do God's will.

Words and good intentions are not enough.
Perseverance is built on our good works.
Let us be witnesses, faithful and true.
Obey the Commandments. That's what we can do.

Eric Burdon and the Animals sang,
"I'm just a soul whose intentions are good.
Lord, please don't let me be misunderstood."
I am not a misunderstood genius.

Coach Joe Yonto used to say, "Talk is cheap."
His 1961 team was 10-0.

Jesus Healed the Centurion's Servant

Luke 7:6-10

The centurion built a synagogue.
He had respect for the people and Christ.
Closeness to God leads to heart expansion.
Everybody can come to Jesus Christ.

Faith and humility lead to Jesus.
The centurion felt most unworthy.
He approached Jesus with humility.
Christ praised the centurion for his faith.

His confession of his unworthiness
Made him worthy to have his servant healed.
Since Christ was in the centurion's heart,
Jesus did not need to enter his house.

When we recite the centurion's prayer,
We are prepared to receive Communion.

Jesus Christ Forgave a Sinful Woman

Luke 7:36-50

Jesus, Simon, and a sinful woman
Had a meal together in Simon's house.
Simon did not show common courtesy.
The people thought Jesus was a prophet.

Simon thought Jesus Christ was a teacher.
Jesus showed Simon that He was much more.
Jesus knew hidden things. He could read a
Person's thoughts. He knew about the woman.

Christ could forgive sins because He was God.
Forgiveness and love are quite connected.
We show our love for God; He forgives us.
Faith is what saves and love manifests faith.

Jesus forgave the woman; she had faith.
Her humility was the deal maker.

Jesus Used Parables in His Teaching

Luke 8:4-15

Luke reported thirty-two parables.
This passage is about the seed sower.
Jesus Christ used parables all the time.
They show clear thinking for the listeners.

The seed does not grow when there's temptation.
There's no fruit in a pleasure-focused life.
Fruit thrives in honest determination.
This is a call to lead a sober life.

Let's focus minds and hearts on God's Kingdom.
Worldly pleasures are seeds in thorns that choke.
Honest and good hearts produce worthwhile fruit.
Human virtues produce the Spirit fruit:

Faithfulness, gentleness, goodness, kindness,
Joy, love, patience, peace, self-control. Amen.

Patrick McCaskey

Jesus Taught the Parable of the Lamp

Luke 8:16-18

When we take the teaching of Jesus Christ
To heart, we become the light of the world.
Let's help other people get to Heaven.
Lighted paths lead to our eternal life.

Sports Faith recognizes people who are
Successful in sports while leading lives that
Are exemplary. We honor athletes,
Coaches, and teams on Pentecost Vigil.

The common denominator of Sports
Faith Hall of Famers is that they think they
Don't deserve it. So, I offer a Jack
Benny quote. "I really don't deserve this
Award. Then again, I have arthritis
And I don't deserve that either." Amen.

Jesus Spoke About His Passion and Death

Luke 9:43-45

After the Transfiguration, Jesus
Told the disciples about His passion
And death, but the disciples missed the point.
They did not have the grace of the Spirit.

Christ's passion and death were in the future.
Luke wrote about Christ's humiliation,
Not about His glorification and
The victory of His resurrection.

Love the cross; identify with Jesus.
Crucify yourself through self-denial.

When my wife, Gretchen, and I do our chores
Together, we are like Torvill and Dean.
They were a very dramatic figure
Skating pair in the winter Olympics.

Patrick McCaskey

Jesus Taught the Apostles Through Children

Luke 9:46-50

Since the apostles had a flawed outlook,
Jesus Christ taught them to be like children.
The apostles had worldly ambition.
A child simply wants to get to heaven.

Do not praise yourself; always be humble.
Do not seek your own glory. Do not have
Evil intentions against your neighbor.
Don't fill your soul with any recklessness.

Let's find room for all people in our hearts.
Rejoice when others are doing good works.
Let's ask God to give them abundant grace.
Then we will not have to do as much work.

If I am the last one to leave after
Mass, then I won't have to be the doorman.

Jesus Made His Way to Jerusalem

Luke 9:51-56

When Jesus traveled to Jerusalem,
He was leading the way to salvation.
The Samaritans had rejected Him.
Jesus knew that He would be crucified.

The disciples wanted to get revenge.
That was not the mission of Jesus Christ.
He came to save people, not destroy them.
Work for God should never be violent.

Here is what we can learn from Saint Ambrose.
True virtue does not have room for vengeance.
Charity does not have room for anger.
Weakness should not be treated with harshness.

Jesus did not sing "Zip-A-Dee-Doo-Dah."
James Baskett sang that in "Song of the South."

Patrick McCaskey

Parable of the Good Samaritan

Luke 10:25-37

A lawyer stood Jesus Christ to the test.
Christ answered his question with two questions.
The lawyer answered very correctly.
Then the lawyer asked another question.

Jesus Christ answered with a parable.
He wanted us to be compassionate.
He symbolized the good Samaritan.
Adam was the man among the robbers.

Thieves left the man on the side of the road.
All of his wounds would be healed in the Church.

Johnny Carson asked Ed McMahon, "What's it
Like to be half Catholic and half Jewish?"
Ed McMahon said, "You still have to go to
Confession, but you can bring your lawyer."

Martha and Mary Welcomed Jesus Christ

Luke 10:38-42

Martha was quite busy with household chores.
Mary listened intently to Jesus.
Martha had many things to attend to.
Mary concentrated on Jesus Christ.

Martha symbolizes activity.
Mary symbolizes contemplation.
Both vocations are very important.
We have to pray and be responsible.

We contemplate the supernatural.
We love our neighbors because we love God.
All these things are a preview of Heaven.
All of our actions converge on Jesus.

While I played with a baby granddaughter,
Her other grandfather did the dishes.

Jesus Prayed; Then He Taught His Disciples

Luke 11:1-4

After Jesus had prayed, His disciples
Asked Him to teach them how to pray like Him.
He taught them to pray to God the Father.
This showed that we are the children of God.

Jesus became man to save the sinners.
We should love God; He has forgiven us.
We ask God for the right amount to eat.
A healthy meal is much more than a treat.

After I had read about fifteen Scott
Hahn books, I became convinced to go to
Mass and Communion nearly every day.
Live the Gospel to be worthy of it.

We ask for strength to deal with temptation
Since temptation is part of life on Earth.

Saint Basil

Jesus Taught the Effectiveness of Prayer

Luke 11:5-13

Prayers of petition are not sedition.
For a good story pray for God's glory.
When we don't swear, we have effective prayer.

Sometimes praying may seem like pestering,
But praying is better than festering.
Pray with folded hands without gesturing.

The Holy Spirit is the greatest gift.
We can count on Him to give us a lift.
We have confidence to call God Father
And participate in the grace of Christ.

Please, please do not just take my word for it.
Saint Basil wrote about it; I read it.

My father asked us to pray for his hair.
I try to avoid a chocolate éclair.

Jesus Expressed Himself with Strong Language

Luke 11:37-41

A Pharisee invited Christ to dine.
Jesus felt that it would be mighty fine.
Much later, Johnny Cash sang "Walk the Line."

The Pharisee was quite surprised to see
That Jesus did not wash his hands with glee.
In fact, He did not wash his hands at all.
The Pharisee did not hear Heaven call.

From the Navarre Bible notes, we know that
Christ said why His teaching was rejected:
Hypocrisy cloaked in legalism.

In an episode of "Seinfeld," George said
About the men's room, "Regardless of what
I need to do I use a stall." Kramer
Responded, "So, you're a stall man." Amen.

Christ Advocated Justice and Mercy

Luke 11:42-46

The Pharisees caused others to transgress.
The harder they tried, they accomplished less.
They did not know quite what they were doing.
This was way before Marshall McLuhan.

The precedents are justice and God's love.
When you are in the line, please do not shove.
Do not be concerned with things external.
Let us concentrate on things eternal.

The Pharisees did not show the right way.
They caused the faithful to wander astray.
Let us check what is in a person's heart.
Let us hope we will not have a false start.

It is important to take a shower.
Christ did not want any earthly power.

Jesus Showed That the Pharisees Were Fools

Luke 11:47-54

Lawyers were Law doctors; they were called scribes.
They interpreted the Law for their tribes.
They were not concerned about any libel.
They were not the heroes of the Bible.

The rebuke of Jesus was quite severe.
It was way too early for Paul Revere.
He helped us to be free of British rule.
Longfellow's poem has been taught in school.

Abel and the prophets died as martyrs.
It is good to have schools that have charters.
Jesus's attitude we should imitate.
When you are in doubt do not hesitate.

Will Shakespeare wrote, "To get disorder in
Society, let's kill all the lawyers."

Christ Gave Instructions
to His Disciples

Luke 12:1-7

In the presence of many thousands, Jesus
Gave instructions to His twelve disciples.
He said it for all of His followers.
They would also receive persecution.

The hypocrisy of the Pharisees
Would work against the disciples and us.
Every Christian would face accusations.
Christ asked them to be steadfast and fearless.

Providential God will take care of us
Even when we play Providence High School.

When my sons were each Loyola freshmen,
My son, Ed, pitched very well against them.
My son, Tom, threw four touchdowns against them.
My son, Jim, had eight tackles against them.

Endowed with the Wisdom of the Spirit

Luke 12:8-12

From the Navarre Bible notes, we know that
What Jesus taught the disciples has been
"Echoed in the words of many martyrs"
Like Saint Ignatius and Saint Polycarp.

From Saint Thomas More's daughter, Margaret,
We know that he consoled his good daughter.
He knew that God would not let him be lost.
With good hope he was committed to God.

In good faith he trusted God Almighty.
He did not want his daughter to worry
About what would happen to him on earth.
Whatever happened was the will of God.

"What so ever that be, seme it never
So bad in sight, it shall dede be the best."

Patrick McCaskey

Jesus Christ Taught the Need for Vigilance

Luke 12:35-38

In the year two thousand one, my booklet
"Gird Your Loins" was printed. Seven Bible
Quotes were on the dedication page,
Including Luke chapter twelve verse thirty-five.

"Gird your loins and light your lamps and be like
Servants who await their master's return
From a wedding, ready to open
Immediately when he comes and knocks."

We should gird our loins and keep our lamps lit.
Jesus Christ told parables. I follow
Jesus. So, I write essays and poems.

We should be prepared to die every day.
Our eternal journey could start today.
Let us always be ready. Ready break.

Jesus Explained the Steward Parable

Luke 12:39-48

Christ talked about responsibility.
The faithful souls and the ignorant would
Be judged differently from the lazy,
The calculating, the noncompliant.

Duties of life can lead to holiness.
The Spirit of God leads to sanctity.
Let's worship God in spirit and in truth.
Jesus was poor, humble, and cross-bearing.

Everyone has different chores and gifts.
Charity arouses hope and good works.
Let's act with courage and humility.
Jesus Christ washed the feet of His apostles.

My grandfather overslept and missed the
Eastland. Sometimes it's okay to be late.

Repentance and the Fig Tree Parable

Luke 13:1-9

Events might be a call to repentance.
Every event can help us turn to God.
This even applies to planting new sod.
Photosynthesis is not circumstance.

Over and over and over again,
We can sure be forgiven of our sin.
We can get help from Lassie and Rin Tin Tin.
They can rescue us and help us to win.

Let's repent to avoid eternal death.
I have a friend whose name is Kutas, Beth.
Her son, Jon's, bar mitzvah party was at
Soldier Field. When he danced, he did not yield.

Everyone danced. There was much joy and glee.
The whole event was a great victory.

The Mustard Seed and Leaven Parables

Luke 13:18-21

Jesus told parables for those in need.
The mustard seed is not a weed; take heed.
It's small, but it can become a tall tree.
We're taught to genuflect on the right knee.

Jesus taught the disciples to have faith.
The Church would grow in spite of everything.
The disciples were the weakest of men.
They received great power and the Church spread.

The parable of leaven leads us to
Heaven. Light leaven makes many bread loaves.
The power of God transforms anything.

I've gone from detention to the school board.
Some school board meetings feel like detention.
I'm a Judeo Christian Catholic.

Jesus Christ Left
the Pharisees Speechless

Luke 14:1-6

The Pharisees worked hard on the Sabbath.
They carefully planned to trap Jesus Christ.
They invited Him to dinner. Then they
Brought in a man who had been quite ill.

Would Jesus cure the man on the sabbath?
Yes, He did. He also said that it was
Okay to pull an ass or an ox out
Of a well on the sabbath, happy day.

Jesus Christ showed basic human concern.
He humbly showed charity and justice.
Religious freedom is for everyone
Because every person has dignity.

God is with us every day of the week.
Crosby sang "Sunday, Monday, or Always."

Jesus Exemplified Humility

Luke 14: 7-11

Seeking the highest place leads to disgrace.
Being humble avoids a big tumble.
Being exalted tastes like a malted.
It's calorie free for both you and me.

Humility helps us to be stress free.
It is a virtue that we should pursue.
Let's walk in the truth like Esther and Ruth.
Living by ourselves leads to misery.

At a dinner party don't be smarty.
It's a long drive home if feelings were hurt.
It's best to give praise to your lovely wife.
Then you can drive home without any strife.

I try to sit in the front pew because
I am trying to ace the course. Amen.

Conditions for Following Jesus Christ

Luke 14:25-33

Jesus was much more than a great teacher.
He was the ultimate, greatest preacher.
Put Jesus Christ first or expect the worst.
God elected Jacob; he chose Rachel.

Take God's side. In compromise, do not hide.
Love God before relatives and strangers.
The builder should be able to finish.
The king should win or negotiate peace.

Saint Gregory the Great was never late.
Since he was on time, we can be sublime.
He taught us to use the things of this world
But desire to take the heavenly things.

My father used to say, "When I am the
Lector, there's usually a big crowd."

Lazarus and the Rich Man Parable

Luke 16:19-31

A rich man lived a life of luxury.
He did not see Lazarus as neighbor.
Lazarus was poor and thus overlooked.
He was another self of the rich man.

The rich man was deaf to the voice of God.
Even though God spoke quite clearly to him.
God spoke well through Moses and the prophets.
The rich man and his brothers did not hear.

The soul does indeed survive after death.
There will be a holy day of judgment.
Prosperity does not mean probity.
Misfortune is not punishment for sin.

Cardinal George used to say, if we give
To the poor, we won't have to go to Hell.

Patrick McCaskey

The Pharisee and the Tax Collector

Luke 18:9-14

Pharisee does rhyme with humility,
But this Pharisee was self-satisfied.
He did not kneel and his prayers were not true.
He listed the things that he was doing right.

The tax collector knelt; he was humble.
He repented; he put his trust in God.
Here is something from a Saint Augustine
Sermon, "Man is a beggar before God."

When this passage was the Gospel, my dad
Did a parody of the Pharisee.
"Lord, I thank thee that I am not like the
Other men: dirty, unshaven, and late."

What is to be learned from this parable?
Pray with constancy and humility.

Douai Abbey Cross

Patrick McCaskey

JOHN

Nicodemus Visited Jesus Christ

John 3:1-8

Nicodemus was quite intelligent.
He was a man of reason, not treason.
He was curious, not furious.
He constantly searched for the truth, not Ruth.

Reason was not enough to understand
The Divine. He also needed grace and
Humility. He learned from Jesus Christ.
Nicodemus could attain salvation.

He knew about his mortal birth on earth.
He learned about life for eternity.
Birth on earth is a great start. Baptism
Is for entry to the kingdom of God.

Nicodemus rhymes with John Doremus.
He did radio and airplane programs.

Nicodemus Had a Worthwhile Visit

John 3:7-15

Jesus Christ explained to Nicodemus
That he needed faith to understand what
He was being told. He was not too old.
He was a young dog. He could learn new tricks.

Jesus taught him salvation history.
Heaven is the ultimate victory.
When Jesus would later be on the cross,
Look on Him with faith and don't get a loss.

Let us be grateful for Vatican II.
We cannot get free from sin on our own.
"All have need of Christ, who is the model,
...liberator, savior, ...giver of life."

Believe in Jesus; get eternal life.
Here on earth, I have a wonderful wife.

Pope Saint John Paul II

Christ Had a Visit with Nicodemus

John 3:14-21

Moses raised a snake in the wilderness.
Jesus Christ was crucified on the cross.
The Israelites got out of Egypt.
Jesus Christ rose from the dead on Easter.

The death of Jesus Christ expressed God's love.
We have the opportunity to respond.
To understand the divine, we need grace
And Baptism from the Holy Spirit.

Saint John Paul II wrote about salvation
Theology. We have to suffer to
Obtain liberation from the devil.
This is the true meaning of salvation.

When a poster at a game read John three
Sixteen, it was not about Madden's weight.

Saint John the Baptist
Bore Witness Again

John 3:22-30

John the Baptist said that he was a friend
Of the bridegroom, his cousin, Jesus Christ.
John the Baptist had quite a special role,
But Jesus Christ was much more important.

John the Baptist was full of joy because
Jesus had already begun to act.
He had called many people to follow
Him and many people had responded.

John the Baptist was faithful and humble.
He felt compelled to disappear after
The Messiah, Jesus Christ, had arrived.
Saint John told others to follow Jesus.

Saint John set a wonderful example.
It's not about us. It's about Jesus.

Jesus Christ Revealed His Divinity

John 3:31-36

Jesus Christ could reveal God the Father
To us because He is The Son of God.
God created one perfect person, Christ.
The Son of God is unsurpassable.

Let's thank God every day for what Jesus
Did and said. He was divinely human.
He, His Father, and The Holy Spirit
Are the ultimate collaborators.

When it is time for me to apply for
Heaven, I hope that God will say to me,
"Come on in Kid. You accepted My Son.
You also did well on your SATs."

Incarnation is for every nation.
Let's do God's will without hesitation.

Christ Cured a Man Who Had Been Paralyzed

John 5:1-16

The pool of Bethzatha was on the out-
skirts of Jerusalem. Many people
Congregated there. One man had been
Ill for thirty-eight years. Jesus cured him.

Jesus acted with the power of God.
He was able to forgive people's sins.
Jesus said that sin is the true evil.
After forgiveness, do not sin again.

Doing the dishes is more fun than white
Washing a fence. I am the loader. If
You know the dishwashers' mission statement,
You can help. "Bring order out of chaos."

God rested on the seventh day. He did
Not create anything new. He maintained.

The Authority of the Son of God

John 5:17-30

After God had created the world, He
Was still active. Christ worked with His Father.
The Holy Spirit worked with Them also.
They kept cooperating and working.

The Father and the Son were equal and
Distinct. The Holy Spirit was also.
Jesus Christ did not exceed His Father.
The Father sent His Son to do His will.

When the Bears won the nineteen eighty-
five championship, there was great cooperation among management, coaches,
And players. Everyone worked together.

Let us work for competition on the
Field and cooperation off the field.

Christ Explained:
Four Witnesses Vouched for Him

John 5:31-47

Jesus did not testify for His cause.
He had four witnesses to vouch for Him:
John the Baptist, the works that Jesus did,
God the Father, and the Holy Scriptures.

Jesus invited people to study
Scripture. They would find an explanation
For what He said and did. The prophets had
Proclaimed that Jesus would come and save us.

Christ pointed out three things that prevented
People from seeing Him as Messiah.
They did not love God; they desired glory;
And their Scripture reading was prejudiced.

Better attitudes help us discover
Christ. Humility leads to good vision.

Christ Miraculously Walked on Water

John 6:16-21

The Disciples did not comprehend Christ.
They could not understand the miracle walk.
Their faith was strengthened when Christ did talk.
Jesus said to them, "Do not be afraid."

The Disciples rowed some three or four miles.
They were Christians, but not Olympians.
With Christ in the boat, they reached land quickly.
When Christ was with them, they were not sickly.

This boat could be a symbol of the Church.
There would be a lot of difficulties.
Jesus promised to always aid the Church.
The Church needed to be firm in the faith.

When Seamus Heaney was on his deathbed,
He said to his wife, "Do not be afraid."

The Discourse of Jesus Christ Continued

John 6:30-35

The people asked Jesus Christ for a sign
Like the manna their ancestors received.
Jesus said the manna was from Heaven.
He also said He was the bread of life.

When Jesus was a baby, the Magi
Gave Him gifts of gold, frankincense, and myrrh.
When Jesus was an adult, He gave gifts
Of faith, Eucharist, and eternal life.

Christ was the only one who could give these
Gifts. He was everyone's superior.
He solved the Incarnation mystery.
Jesus became man while still being God.

The discourse was a great conversation.
Everybody could attain salvation.

Disciples Reacted to the Discourse

John 6:60-69

Although outlandish, Jesus expected
His Disciples to believe what He said.
The Eucharistic mystery was solved.
They suffered from some incredulity.

What Jesus revealed was not sensible.
Their faith would be strengthened in the future.
The Resurrection made them believers.
They would then become senior achievers.

An act of faith would lead to divine grace.
The Messiah was here, no more the chase.
Peter knew that what Jesus said was true
Because the words came from God Almighty.

Peter and his successors expressed their
Faith in the Divinity of Jesus.

Jesus Evoked Various Reactions

John 7:40-53

The prophet Micah had predicted the
Messiah would be born in Bethlehem.
John the Evangelist knew that Jesus
Had been born there, the city of David.

People who had not seen the miracles
Of Jesus but who had heard Him preach felt
That He spoke in a most powerful way.
They said, "No man ever spoke like this man."

Some people who had seen the miracles
And who had heard Him speak were opponents.
Believers tried to help unbelievers.
The unbelievers were too hard-hearted.

The title of Josh McDowell's first book
Is "Evidence That Demands a Verdict."

Jesus Said That the Father Had Sent Him

John 8:21-30

When the authorities rejected Christ,
He warned them that He would leave and return
To Heaven. They would continue to hope
For a Messiah. They would not find Him.

Jesus was the Messiah. They could not
Follow Him because they did not believe
In Him. Jesus was the expression of
God's faithfulness, even though we're sinners.

God gave His Son for us. He showed mercy.
Jesus gave His life to free us from sin.
The passion, death, and resurrection of
Jesus gave us a chance for salvation.

The Cross of Jesus became a royal throne.
He lifted us up to get to heaven.

Patrick McCaskey

Jesus is the Truth; He Will Set Us Free

John 8:31-42

Jesus requires more than enthusiasm.
Faith in Jesus means true discipleship.
To know Jesus Christ is to know the truth.
Then we are no longer enslaved to sin.

Jesus leads us to authentic freedom.
We are free for salvation history.
We are free to seek God's infinite love.
We are free from all forms of slavery.

Jesus cured addictions and afflictions.
His ministry had no contradictions.
Jesus Christ gave us the chance for freedom.
We are eligible for God's Kingdom.

God sent Christ to us. If we accept Christ,
Then we are the children of God. Amen.

Jesus Christ Is the Gateway to Heaven

John 10:1-10

David was a shepherd who became a king.
Christ was a king who became a shepherd.
Jesus fulfilled the ancient prophecies
Of Jeremiah and Ezekiel.

The illustration of Jesus as the
Good Shepherd shows God's love for each of us.
Like the Waltons at bedtime, He calls all
Of us: "Good night beloved; follow Me."

Jesus speaks through the Church; let us listen
To the priests, the cardinals, and the pope.
If they say something that we do not like
Let's not mope. Let us remember Saint George.

Saint George slayed dragons and rescued maidens.
Let's be chivalrous and charitable.

Jesus Said He and the Father Are One

John 10:22-30

Jesus used the image of the shepherd.
He spoke about the mystery of God.
He and the Father have divine natures.
He and the Father are distinct Persons.

Jesus Christ gave up His life for His sheep.
Here's something from Saint Thomas Aquinas.
If we open our eyes, we're able to see.
If we close our eyes, we prevent sunlight.

The Father eternally begot Christ.
The Son is eternally Word of God.
Father, Son, and Holy Spirit are One.
There is Unity in the Trinity.

My sons Ed, Tom, Jim are distinct persons.
Yet, they are great brothers to each other.

The Death of Christ Led to the Church

John 11:45-57

Some believed in Jesus. Others did not.
The death of Christ fulfilled the prophecies.
He gathered the believers together.
The Church was united throughout the world.

The will of God is fulfilled in the Church.
He created human nature as one.
He sent His beloved Son, His appointed
Heir, to be preacher, teacher, and Savior.

The Church is universal, one body.
It transcends borders. We're all God's children.
Christ went with His disciples to Ephraim.
It might have been close to Jerusalem.

The Passover reference set the scene.
Christ is the definitive Passover.

Patrick McCaskey

Mary of Bethany Anointed Christ

John 12:1-11

After Jesus had raised Lazarus from
The dead, He made a follow-up house call.
Christ visited Lazarus, Martha, and
Mary at their home. They ate together.

They had made a meal for Him. Martha served.
Lazarus and others sat with Jesus.
Mary anointed Jesus with a costly
Ointment. Judas soundly criticized her.

Jesus told Judas to leave her alone.
Ointment could be used for His burial.
Mary responded to the love of Christ.
She was magnanimous and gave her all.

Jesus indirectly announced His coming
Death. There would not be time for much planning.

Christ Announces His Glorification

John 12:20-33

From the Navarre Bible commentary,
We know that "Jesus...is...a seed that" dies
"And thereby produces abundant fruit."
He was humbled; then He was glorified.

Every suffering and contradiction
Shares Christ's cross. We're redeemed and exalted.
When we die to ourselves without a thought
To our own comfort or desires and plans,
We're supernaturally effective.

Christ fell three times on the walk to His death.
I threw three interceptions in one game.
Jesus rose from the dead to His glory.
I made Catholic All-American.

There are ten syllables in every line.

God's Glory is More Important Than Praise

John 12:44-50

In this passage, John summarized quite well.
Jesus was the One whom His Father sent.
Father and the Son are One but distinct.
Christ is the Life and the Light of the world.

We will be judged by what we accept or
Reject about what Jesus revealed.
Jesus came to give us eternal life.
He died for us. He is the final Judge.

My grandfather said to an official,
"No man is completely worthless. You can
Always serve as a horrible example."
He was also a man of faith and prayer.

At the end of his life, he stopped swearing.
He thanked God for his long, wonderful life.

Jesus Washed the Feet of His Disciples

John 13:1-15

Jesus Christ came to serve and not be served.
He washed the Disciples' feet to show this.
Saint Peter did not understand Jesus.
Jesus exemplified humility.

If you want to follow Jesus Christ, you
Must humbly serve and be a foot-washer.
Servants have spiritual maturity.
Jesus Christ always did His Father's will.

Christ redeemed us from slavery to sin.
He passed over from this world to Heaven.
Since the Disciples would practice virtue,
They would follow Jesus into Heaven.

Let's give up any pride and ambition.
Let's strive and thrive to be the most humble.

Jesus Was an Example of Service

John 13:16-20

Jesus Christ always did His Father's will.
He even died on a cross for others.
Jesus said that if we imitate Him,
No one can take away our happiness.

If we give up our pride and ambition,
Peace and joy will come to our fruition.
Jesus said that Judas would betray Him.
Apostles saw His prediction come true.

They knew Jesus had divine foreknowledge.
Old Testament scriptures found fulfilment.
Jesus Christ is the One who is God's Son.
Being with God in Heaven He has won.

My mother and my wife make many meals.
They deserve to eat in a restaurant.

Christ Foretold the Treachery of Judas

John 13:21-33, 36-38

After Jesus had washed the feet of His
Disciples, including Judas, Jesus
Predicted that one of them would betray
Him. He gave a good morsel to Judas.

Judas was tempted. Jesus said to him,
"What you are going to do, do quickly."
The other Disciples thought that Jesus
Had sent Judas to go for feast supplies.

The morsel was a sign of friendship, an
Invitation to reject temptation.
This sin took place in the darkness of night.
The darkness did not defeat the True Light.

Coach Abe Gibron used to say, "You dropped me
Like a rat deserting a sinking ship."

To Know Jesus is to Know His Father

John 14:7-14

When Jesus died, He left the Apostles.
Jesus Christ went to be with His Father.
Christ is God; He and His Father are One.
Christ said He was the way to His Father.

Christ became man to do His Father's will.
Jesus was the face of God Almighty.
Everything that Jesus Christ said and did
Was a Revelation of His Father.

Christ gave His Apostles clear direction.
God's salvation would become known through them.
They would perform miracles in Christ's name.
Sanctify through preaching and sacraments.

Ask Jesus for salvation and Heaven.
He will say yes for what will get us there.

Jesus Christ Promised the Holy Spirit

John 14:27-31

Christ gave the gift of the Holy Spirit.
It was wrapped with peace. Everyone could be
Reconciled with God and everybody.
The peace that was sent transcended the world.

God was greater than Christ's human nature.
Jesus ascended to the right hand of God.
They are both equal in divinity.
Holy Spirit rounds out the Trinity.

The world involved those who rejected Christ.
The devil became the prince of darkness.
My fall on the Church parking lot dark ice
Was a chance to be declared a martyr.

There is no vacation from vocation.
God gave me a gift; I pass it along.

Patrick McCaskey

Jesus is the Vine, We are the Branches

John 15:1-8

The night before Jesus died, He spoke well.
He is the vine; His Father grows the vine.
We receive tribulations and temptations.
They make us stronger; we serve God longer.

My earthly father once said to me, "It's
Up to you but you're doing it all wrong."
Accountability, encouragement
Help us get pruned of our ungodliness.

When we are with Jesus Christ, we sin less,
We do holy works, and we help others.
Mass and the Sacraments, Bible study,
And daily devotions keep us attuned.

The Holy Trinity helps us stay pruned.
When Christ is our vine, we are mighty fine.

Poems About the Gospel II

Pope Saint Gregory

Christ's Followers Expect
a Hostile World

John 15:18-21

Jesus Christ gave a mandate: accept Him.
Do not compromise with the worldly wise.
When sin is triumphant be eloquent.
Evil is the in the room elephant.

Jesus received worldly persecution.
The Apostles were persecuted too.
Evil people are afraid of the light.
Christ-led people can keep up the good fight.

Here's something from Saint Gregory the Great.
Perverse hostility could be our praise.
Let's increase our tithe if we get a raise.
We are God's stewards; it is not too late.

We are not here to please God's enemies.
We are here to live the Holy Gospel.

Jesus Ascended and Sent the Spirit

John 16:5-11

Jesus would not desert His Disciples.
He would ascend to Heaven and send the
Holy Spirit to lead the Disciples.
Then they would understand what Christ revealed.

The Spirit would work through the Disciples.
They would convince those who did not believe.
Sinners would become righteous and believe
In Jesus who never committed sin.

Christ sits in glory at His Father's side.
Believers receive the great gifts of God.
The faithful will not be condemned to Hell.
The worst part of Dante's Hell is extreme cold.

"Divine Comedy" had a good ending.
An important part was Christ's ascending

Patrick McCaskey

Pentecost Light

Unbroken Succession Through the Spirit

John 16:12-15

Jesus Christ revealed the truth. The Holy
Spirit helped the Apostles understand.
The Apostles were lost until Pentecost.
The Paraclete provides love to the Church.

The three divine Persons are equal.
Remember Saint Patrick and the shamrock.
Father Hesburgh was in many meetings.
Before each he prayed, "Come Holy Spirit."

When we ask for the Spirit, He is there.
He is even there when we do not ask.
Persecutions and trials don't dishearten.
Let's turn difficulties to good purpose.

If I were a friend of Job, I would try
To provide respectful comic relief.

The Apostles Did Not Understand Christ

John 16:16-20

Jesus told His Apostles about His
Death and Resurrection. They were baffled.
They would be upset. They would be joyful.
Jesus would rise. They would get to Heaven.

Christ said something. They did not understand.
They repeated what He had said to them.
He knew that they did not know what He meant.
He repeated what He had said to them.

When Coach Wooden corrected a player,
He used the same tone of voice more than once.
The player eventually behaved.
Coach Wooden was a great Christian teacher.

The Apostles grew to understand Christ.
Teacher Wooden won ten championships.

Christ Told the Apostles to Ask for Joy

John 16:23b-28

In effect, Christ said to His Apostles,
"When you have questions, go ask My Father."
God would answer in the name of Jesus.
The answer received would make them joyful.

After the Resurrection of Jesus,
He would speak plainly to His Apostles.
"Plain Speaking" was about Harry Truman.
He was gruff and pragmatic and truthful.

The Apostles would understand God's love.
God sent His Son and He died for our sins.
The Cross was no longer a mystery.
It was part of salvation history.

Joy Piccolo O'Connell is a joy.
She knew Brian Piccolo as a boy.

Patrick McCaskey

Christ Spoke Plainly; the Disciples Believed

John 16:29-33

The Disciples had faith because Jesus
Knew everything and He read every heart.
Jesus predicted that they would leave Him.
This would console them after He would rise.

When the Disciples would have trials and errors,
They would remember to be of good cheer.
So it is for all of the believers.
We have grace to be cheerful achievers.

Let's work for God's glory and not our own.
In this way we will never be alone.
Prayer is a spiritual telephone.
The Bears were quite blessed to have Doug Buffone.

Believe and achieve and please don't deceive.
May God crown us with a heavenly wreath.

Jesus the Son Prayed to God the Father

John 17:1-11

Christ prayed a prayer that no one else could pray.
He asked His Father to glorify His
Holy human nature and to accept
His sacrifice on the cross for Heaven.

Christ was obedient to His Father.
Jesus obeyed the redemption mandate.
His death made His Father known to all.
We get to go to Heaven thanks to Christ.

Christ's divinity saved humanity.
His humanity gave us dignity.
In Heaven, knowledge of God will be full.
We can trust Saint Augustine to be right.

Jesus prayed for us and He died for us.
That is quite a lot more than we deserve.

Patrick McCaskey

Before Christ Was Buried,
His Side Was Pierced

John 19:31-37

The soldiers did not break the legs of Christ.
They knew that Jesus was already dead.
Jesus Christ was/is the true Paschal Lamb.
Jesus took away the sin of the world.

When the soldiers pierced the side of Jesus,
Blood and water flowed. These are the figures
Of the sacraments and the Church itself.
Church Doctor Augustine is right again.

Here is a great quote from Vatican II.
"The origin and growth of the Church are
Symbolized by the blood and water which
Flowed from the open side of...Jesus" Christ.

When Jesus Christ won salvation on the
Cross, God's redemption promise was fulfilled.

Jesus Appeared to Mary Magdalene

John 20:11-18

Mary Magdalene searched for Jesus Christ.
A depth of love for Him burned in her heart.
She alone stayed close to the tomb of Christ.
All of the Disciples had gone away.

Mary looked for Jesus to be with Him.
She hoped He had not been taken away.
She stayed close; she was the first to see Him.
Perseverance was justly rewarded.

Jesus Christ called her name. She knew His voice.
Mary first witnessed the Resurrection.
Then she shared the news with alacrity.
The Disciples would become His brethren.

Jesus said to Mary, "Do not hold me."
He had to leave her and go to Heaven.

Patrick McCaskey

Christ Loved John Who Had a Very Long Life

John 21:20-25

Saint John was the last Apostle to die.
He was the beloved of Jesus Christ.
The witness of John helps us to carry on.
All his reports are worthy of belief.

John's Gospel is Holy Spirit inspired.
His narrative does not make us tired.
His Epistles are worthy of whistles.
The Holy Spirit also inspired those.

Saint John told us what Jesus did and taught.
This helps all of us to do what we ought.
There is still more to learn about Jesus.
He came here to serve and not just please us.

There are many depths for us to explore.
Let us live to love Jesus more and more.

Photo Credits

All photographs are reproduced with permission.

Page	Photo Description	Source
Cover	Rosary Shrine in London, https://flic.kr/p/DYaP11	Fr. Lawrence Lew, O.P.
X	God the Father, Carved tympanum above the entrance to the church of the Carmelite Convent of the Annunciation in Alba de Tormes. https://flic.kr/p/2jdUiRP	Fr. Lawrence Lew, O.P.
5	Jesus Taught Them: Detail from the bronze doors of the Basilica of the Annunciation in Nazareth, the Holy Land, https://flic.kr/p/2mbZyRV.	Fr. Lawrence Lew, O.P.
13	Christ Raises the Daughter of Jarius, Painting by Henry Thomson (1810) in the Tate Britain Gallery, https://flic.kr/p/2m7WfTJ	Fr. Lawrence Lew, O.P.
41	St John Chrysostom, mosaic detail from St Paul within the Walls in Rome, https://flic.kr/p/dam9DC	Fr. Lawrence Lew, O.P.
46	Annunciation Sculpture, Bas relief detail from the pulpit in Santa Maria Novella, Florence, https://flic.kr/p/2kGR5Ct	Fr. Lawrence Lew, O.P.

Page	Photo Description	Source
49	Saint Augustine in the church of San Bernardo alle Terme in Rome. https://www.flickr.com/photos/paullew/7878434370/	Fr. Lawrence Lew, O.P.
86	Benediction in Blackfriars priory church; https://flic.kr/p/87eU4H	Fr. Lawrence Lew, O.P.
88	Saint Joseph the Worker, painting from Salamanca Cathedral, https://flic.kr/p/2kVZ4gj	Fr. Lawrence Lew, O.P.
107	Saint Basil the Great, Stained glass from Cologne Cathedral, https://flic.kr/p/PADBt4	Fr. Lawrence Lew, O.P.
123	Douai Abbey Cross, Photo of the Cross above the choir of Douai Abbey near Reading, England, https://flic.kr/p/2k1jiBp	Fr. Lawrence Lew, O.P.
126	Pope Saint John Paul II, statue of the Saint is in the USCCB building in Washington DC. https://www.flickr.com/photos/paullew/50515233863/	Fr. Lawrence Lew, O.P.
151	Pope Saint Gregory the Great, from St Mary's Episcopal Cathedral in Edinburgh, he is shown directing a schola cantorum. https://flic.kr/p/xSTkhY	Fr. Lawrence Lew, O.P.
154	Pentecost Light at Blackfriars church in Oxford, https://flic.kr/p/6sA3jT	Fr. Lawrence Lew, O.P.

Patrick McCaskey

Patrick McCaskey was born at Saint Francis Hospital in Evanston. He played basketball and baseball for Saint Mary's School in Des Plaines. He played football and ran track for Notre Dame High School in Niles. He ran cross-country and track for Cheshire Academy in Connecticut. Pat's mom and dad had 11 children: 3 girls and 8 boys. His parents encouraged faith, hard work, reading, and a good laugh.

Pat was a contributing editor to the literary magazines at Loyola University in Chicago and Indiana University. He started working for the Chicago Bears in 1974. He went to DePaul University at night during the off-seasons and earned a master's degree.

Pat is a Chicago Bears' Board Member and a Bears' Vice President. He is the Chairman of Sports Faith International which recognizes people who are successful in sports while leading exemplary lives. Sports Faith has a radio station, WSFI, 88.5 FM, which broadcasts in northern Illinois and southern Wisconsin.

Pat and his wife, Gretchen, have three sons: Ed, Tom, and Jim; two daughters in law: Elizabeth and Emily; four granddaughters: Grace, Charlotte, Violet Min, and Madeline; and a grandson, Pat.

Patrick McCaskey

Sporting Chance Press Books
by Patrick McCaskey

Sports and Faith: Stories of the Devoted and the Devout

Sports and Faith: More Stories of the Devoted and the Devout

Pillars of the NFL: Coaches Who Have Won Three or More Championships

Pilgrimage

Worthwhile Struggle

Sportsmanship

Papa Bear and the Chicago Bears' Winning Ways

Poems About the Gospel

Poems About the Gospel II

Tuition Rebate (forthcoming)